Learning activities for ea...

Art from stories, poems and songs

Ann Malpass and Dorothy Tipton

Illustrations by Alison Dexter

Photographs by Zul Mukhida

Contents

A & C Black · London

Introduction

In this book, stories, rhymes and songs provide a starting point for a wide variety of art experiences and activities that take art into all areas of the curriculum. In preparing this book, the authors have considered not only the creative development of the child but also his or her personal and social development. It is important that a child learns *'how to work, play, co-operate with others and function in a group beyond the family'* (SCAA). This book helps to show how art can form part of an integrated programme of learning and contribute to a broad, balanced and purposeful curriculum.

About this book

The book is divided into case studies, each focusing on one of the important 'elements of art' (line, colour, tone, pattern, texture, shape, form and space). The final case study looks at the work of a famous artist, linking together all of these elements and illustrating how they can be used to achieve different effects.

The stories, songs or poems at the start of the case studies have been carefully selected for the links that they can help to make. Some stories will be familiar; others have been chosen because they are likely to be new to the children and the teacher. The books mentioned could be bought or ordered in advance from a library. However, the activity suggestions are flexible and can be adapted to link with other stimuli.

The case studies are not intended to be worked through in any particular order, but where two are linked (for example, *Colour* and *Mixing colour*), it would be helpful to use them together to develop and extend the ideas. Throughout the book we have tried to maintain an awareness of art from other countries as well as recognising the many cultures represented within our own community.

The content of each section is organised under the following headings: Intended learning, Key vocabulary, The activity (which also covers the materials you will need and points for discussion before you start), Assessment, Evidence of the children's learning, Differentiating the activity, Extension activities, Involving Parents and an Example (of an artist's work). Intended outcomes are reflected in the assessment process.

The activities are differentiated to provide all children with opportunities for discussion and creativity. The stages of creative development will vary from child to child, depending on eye-to-hand co-ordination and the child's ability to interpret what has been seen.

Art is a creative process that everyone can experience. The end results within a group will often be very different, but where a challenge has been attempted, much praise should be given. Some of the activities are designed for individual children, others for small groups, and others for whole-class participation.

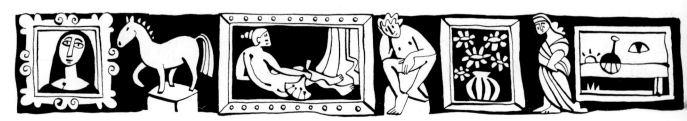

Throughout the book, parents are seen as partners to be welcomed into the classroom to assist with the activities and to give their support. An understanding of a teacher's approach can enable parents to stimulate and support the child's artistic development at home.

For each case study we have included an example of a painting, sculpture or other work of art to reflect the element of art being explored. All the examples we have quoted are well-known and the teacher should be able to find reproductions in general books on art or in poster or post-card form from specialist art shops.

A comprehensive list of special materials required is included in each activity which, combined with the basic list of resources included here, should make preparation and organisation much easier.

Basic list of materials

The following materials should be readily available for any art activity: a selection of drawing equipment, including crayons, charcoal and pastels; a variety of different types of paints; a variety of brushes; card of different colours and thicknesses; different kinds of paper, including cartridge and sugar paper; glue and spreaders; scissors (both right- and left-handed); water pots; mixing palettes; found materials (for example, stones, fir cones, boxes, shells, tubes, lids). It is also important to ensure that the children have aprons or overalls to wear, and that you have a good supply of old newspapers or plastic sheeting to cover work surfaces.

Line

Intended learning

To help children organise lines to create shapes and express movement; to encourage the children to make marks as simple outline drawings; to discuss with the children features of their own drawings and what they represent; to develop their ability to hold, control and manipulate drawing tools.

Responding to: *In the Garden* by Susie Lacome (Walker Books)

Charlie the Clown is working in his garden. The reader is invited to help him find his various gardening tools. The cheerful and clearly-defined drawings in this book provide a good illustration of the use of line.

Key vocabulary

thick, thin, line, long, short, straight, curved line, bold, wavy, draw

The activity

You will need:

a copy of *In the Garden* by Susie Lacome, string, drawing and painting equipment, paper, card, garden tools.

Points for discussion

● Begin by looking together at the cover of *In the Garden*. Talk about how straight and curved lines are used in the picture. Are the shoes curved or straight? Is the wheelbarrow curved or straight? Can you see any wavy lines in the picture?

● Talk about how classroom toys have straight and curved lines. Ask the children to show you some examples.

After the discussion

● Read the story together. Next give each child in the class a piece of string 1 m long. Invite them to make first straight lines, then curved lines in a large space on the floor.

● Encourage the children to think about the sorts of lines they saw in the book, such as the hose pipe, the clown's hat, a daisy shape. Ask them to try to make similar straight and curved shapes with the string, working in pairs. Then enlarge the groups to make more interesting patterns. The children could also be encouraged to draw their patterns on paper, or stick string in patterns onto pieces of sugar paper.

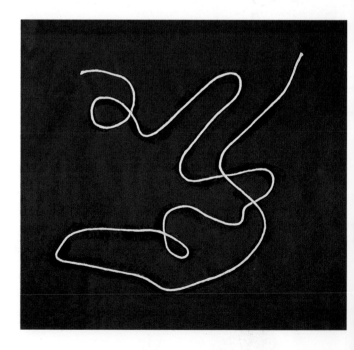

● Set up a display of garden tools (spade, fork, watering can, etc.), then talk about the lines the children can see in these shapes. Ask them to try to draw them using wax crayons, paint, chalk, pastels, thick pencils, etc.

● Use the children's drawings and paintings to create a class book entitled 'The Garden'. Look at the ways in which children have used lines in their work. Encourage them to talk about the different kinds of lines they have used.

Experimenting with making curved, coiled and wavy lines

Assessment

● Can the children make recognisable marks (curved and straight)?

● Can the children talk about their drawings?

● Can they use a range of tools to draw?

● Can they produce recognisable pictures?

● Can the children use line in observational drawings?

● Do the children hold their pencils correctly?

Evidence of the children's learning

The children were surprised at how many different ways they could use their string to make lines. They were keen to explore a variety of shapes and patterns, not just those they had seen in the book. ('Mine looks like a snake; it's wavy.' 'Debra and I have made an arrow with our strings.') They experimented freely with making circles, spirals and crosses, individually, in pairs and in groups.

Differentiating the activity

Some children will need constant reinforcement in drawing lines to develop control. Provide a range of items as templates for them to draw round (for example, pastry cutters, toy railway tracks, lids, plastic plates, large jigsaw pieces). They could also be encouraged to trace images with bold outlines, join dots to create a shape or complete an image (for example, draw a tail on a mouse).

a tractor wheel

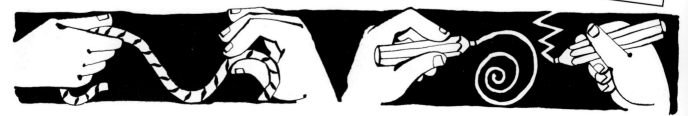

Extension activities

● Fold a sheet of paper in half. Lay pieces of string dipped into paint of different colours on one half of the paper. Fold the other half of the paper over and press it down over the string. Open up the paper to reveal a symmetrical line pattern.

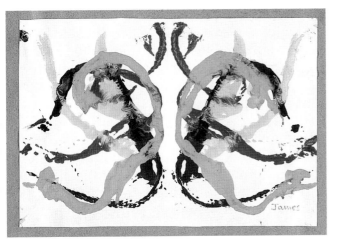

● Look at examples of paintings and drawings from a range of cultures to see how line can be used in a variety of ways in different kinds of art.

● Let the children work in groups of four at a sand tray. Ask the first child to draw a line, the second to add to it, the next to develop the idea and the last to complete it. Ask the children to describe the picture they have made.

● Use coloured construction straws of different sizes to create a line picture.

● More able children could be invited to use pen and ink to create observational drawings.

● Look at pictures or real examples of wheels together (bicycle, car, manual sewing machine, clock, toy truck, wheelbarrow, etc.). Discuss the different lines they can see (the straight spokes and the curved rim), then let the children each choose one to draw.

Below and far left: *observational 'wheel' drawings*

Involving parents

Encourage parents to talk to their children about their drawings and to draw with them. Parents could be asked to point out lines around the home and in the environment, provide their children with pencils and paper, and have stencils available for use at home.

Example

The New Year
by Pablo Picasso

In this painting Picasso uses the minimum of lines to express the idea of a little boy half hiding behind a mask of Father Christmas.

Colour

Intended learning

To introduce and discuss the primary colours (red, blue and yellow), and for the children to learn their names; to learn and understand the term 'primary colours'; for the children to use each colour separately in their work.

Responding to: A A Milne's poem 'Happiness' in *When We Were Very Young* (Methuen)

'John has great big waterproof boots on ...' Children's rainwear is often brightly coloured, so the boots, hat and mackintosh in this poem provide an ideal opportunity for children to experiment with combinations of the three primary colours.

Key vocabulary

red, blue, yellow, sort, use, match, choose, colour

The activity

You will need:

a selection of waterproof hats, coats and wellingtons (in all colours) in a large box, a copy of the poem 'Happiness' by A A Milne, a selection of patterned collage materials in the primary colours, card, scissors, glue.

Points for discussion

Collect examples of different objects in the three colours, and talk about them. Which is your favourite? Why? Are any of these things the same colour? How might these objects be sorted?

After the discussion

● Show the children the box of clothes and ask them to pick out and sort into sets any that are in red, blue or yellow.

● Read the poem 'Happiness' to the children. Ask them what colours they think John might wear (Red hat? Blue coat? Yellow wellingtons?). Pick a child to be 'John' and dress him or her in the appropriate clothes. Then encourage the rest of the group to talk about the clothes 'John' is wearing. Let other children have a turn at being 'John' and choose other combinations of the primary colours to wear.

● Prepare large outline drawings of four children. Divide the class into four groups, and ask each group to decorate one of the outlines with the collage materials in a combination of primary colours. Use these to make a 'Rainy Day' wall picture.

Elizabeth has great
big waterproof
boots on...

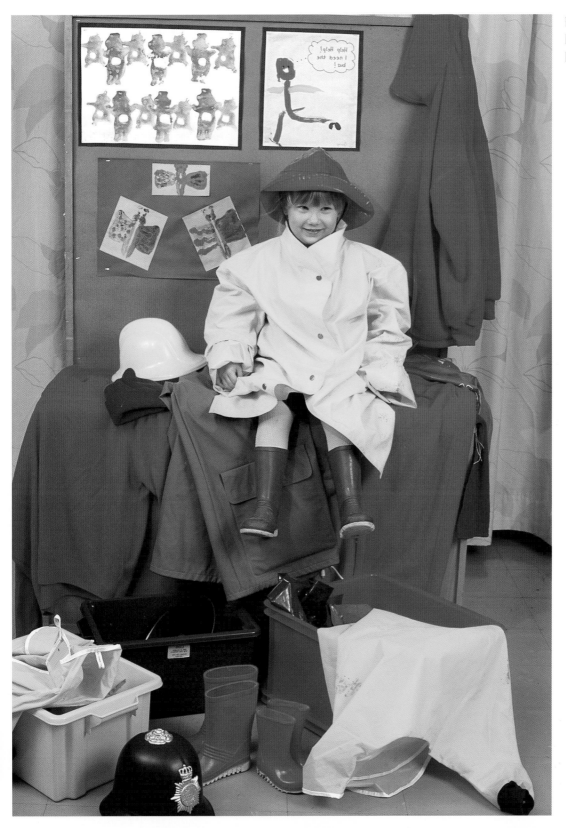

Assessment

● Can the children match and sort the colours red, blue and yellow?

● Can the children select one specific colour?

● Can the children recall the colour names?

● Are they able to use a single colour?

● Can they choose and use the correct colour to represent an object?

● Observe the children's use of the three colours.

Evidence of the children's learning

The children enjoyed the poem. They wanted to learn it by heart and quickly memorised the words. The children all brought their wellingtons in and we had great fun sorting out the red, blue and yellow ones. They began to comment on other examples of the primary colours. Someone said, 'Paddington bear has a blue mac and yellow wellingtons.'

Differentiating the activity

● Some children will take longer than others to recognise and recall the primary colours, and will need constant reinforcement. For example, play skittles using only the three primary colours, and challenge the children to knock down a specific colour; allocate a colour to the children's tables, and encourage them to choose items such as drinking beakers in the correct colour for their table.

● Prepare three postboxes from cardboard boxes and paint them red, blue and yellow.

Give the children each an envelope and ask them to paint it in a primary colour. Then challenge them to post their envelopes in the correct boxes. Ask them to swap envelopes with a friend. Which postbox should they use now?

● Make one day a 'Primary Colour Day', and encourage everyone to wear something red, blue or yellow.

Extension activities

● Create a game of 'Car Snap' by encouraging the children to draw and colour with crayon or paint twelve basic car shapes in each of the primary colours. Let them play the game in small groups.

● With a small group of children, focus on a toy in one of the primary colours, such as a bus, a tractor or a digger. Invite the children to talk about it and its colours, then let them try to paint a picture of it.

● Paint a giant snake in the playground. Arrange red, blue and yellow mats along the snake. Using a colour spinner that shows only red, blue and yellow, ask the children to take turns to spin and then move along the snake to the appropriate colour. Introduce rules such as landing on red means miss a turn, landing on blue means move forward one mat and landing on yellow means go back a square.

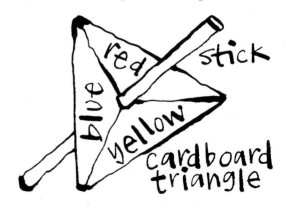

● Make a bingo game by dividing sheets of A4 paper into six sections and asking the children to draw a picture of a red bucket, a blue spade or a yellow sandcastle in each of the sections. Explain that they can choose how many of each item to draw altogether. They could, for example, draw three red buckets, two blue spades and only one yellow sandcastle. Make several cards showing each kind of picture for the caller. Let the children take turns to be the caller and say what is on the cards they are holding. The rest of the group can place a counter on their pictures as the items are called out. The winner is the first child to have put a counter on every picture.

● Cut out house shapes from red, blue or yellow card, then ask the children to decorate them using patterned collage materials for windows, curtains, doors, etc. These could be used as party invitations for a 'Primary Colour Party' complete with party

hats, food and drinks in the primary colours. Check first with parents to ensure that no children are allergic to food colouring.

Involving parents

Ask parents to encourage their children to look for primary colours in the environment, such as red, blue or yellow road signs, red or blue tractors, or yellow diggers.

Example

A Sunday Afternoon on the Island of La Grande Jatte
by Georges Seurat

Seurat used dots of pure colour which from a distance appear to blend together – a technique known as pointillism. If the children look carefully at *A Sunday Afternoon on the Island of La Grande Jatte*, they will be able to identify tiny dots in the primary colours.

Mixing colour

Intended learning

To encourage children to experiment with colours; to show the children how to mix new colours; to help the children to use colours effectively; to teach the colours of the rainbow.

Responding to: *Skyfire* by Frank Asch (Picture Corgi)

'When Bear sees a rainbow for the first time, he thinks the sky is on fire ...' The rainbow in this delightful book should promote discussion about the colours and encourage experimentation in colour-mixing.

Key vocabulary

red, orange, yellow, green, blue, indigo, violet, mix, colour, rainbow, shades, blow, bubbles, change

The activity

You will need:

a collection of leaves, acetate sheets in a range of colours, paint in the primary colours (red, blue and yellow), cartridge paper, a copy of *Skyfire* by Frank Asch, empty plastic ice-cream cartons, bubble mixture, drinking straws, scissors, glue.

Points for discussion

● Talk about the colours that occur in nature. Look at a collection of leaves. Are they all the same colour?

● How many different colours can the children see around them in the classroom?

● How do colours change if we look at them through the coloured acetate?

● Ask if anyone knows the colours that are in a rainbow (red, orange, yellow, green, blue, indigo, violet). The children will probably need to have the words 'indigo' and 'violet' explained to them. Use the following sentence to help them (and you!) remember what the colours are: Rainbows Over Your Garden Bring In Visitors.

After the discussion

● Begin by letting the children experiment with mixing two primary colours. Use this as an opportunity to introduce plenty of colour-related vocabulary (for example, 'Choose two colours and mix them together. What happens? Has anyone made green?'). Explain to the class how to make green, orange and purple.

● Next, let the children try mixing three colours. As they explore mixing paints, help them to discover and talk about why red, blue and yellow cannot be made.

● Read the story of *Skyfire* together, in which Bear sees a rainbow for the first time and thinks the sky is on fire, and so he rushes to put it out with a honey pot filled with water.

● Then explain that the children are going to help you make a wall picture about the story. Start by talking about the things that will need to be included in the frieze (the sky, grass, the sun, a rainbow).

To make a background for the picture, ask the children to create bubble patterns. To do this, mix some bubble mixture with green, purple or

orange paint in large containers such as old ice-cream cartons. The children should blow bubbles in the mixture through a straw then carefully hold a piece of paper over the bubbles as they burst.

Join the sheets of paper to form an appropriate size and shape for the overall picture – use purple for the sky, green for the grass and orange for the sun.

Cut out seven curved strips of paper for the rainbow. Encourage the children to mix paint in the appropriate colours to paint the rainbow strips. Assemble the rainbow and stick it in place on the picture.

Let the children make flowers, leaves and trees to stick on, and ask individual children to make Bear, the bird and the honey pot.

Blowing coloured bubbles to make the background for a frieze that illustrates the story of Bear and the rainbow

Assessment

● Can the children recognise and name the secondary colours (purple, green, orange)?

● Can the children choose the correct paint to create a given colour?

● Are they able to mix the paint successfully?

● Are the children randomly selecting colours to mix or are they choosing specific colours?

Evidence of the children's learning

We observed how nature places different colours together and how all the colours can be found in nature. The children enjoyed trying to find them all. They were surprised when they looked through the acetate and there was much discussion about how colours change.

The colour-mixing was enjoyable and the children were quick to learn how to mix the secondary colours. They soon discovered how mixing all the colours together results in brown! The children were eager to try lots of different paint mixes. Everyone was excited when the bubbles burst in random patterns and they all wanted to have a try.

Differentiating the activity

● Children who have difficulty in recognising and remembering colours can be helped by being involved in sorting activities. Make available coloured paper, pieces of fabric and a range of objects to be sorted into appropriately coloured boxes. Encourage the children by asking questions such as 'Which box does this go in?'. This will help the children to remember the names of the different colours. Matching the same colour objects and a 'Go and find' activity would also help.

● Encourage free expression in the mixing of two colours. If the children cannot name the colours they have made, ask them if they can think of any objects of the same colour.

Extension activities

● Make coloured spinners, using a circle of card with each side divided in half and painted in two colours. Help the children to thread a loop of string through a centre hole and then twist both ends of the loop. When the string is pulled taut it will make the card spin and mix the colours.

● Develop straw-blowing and bubble-painting techniques. Then use individual pieces of work to make bubble-painted book covers, calendars, bookmarks and cards.

● Let the children make butterflies by folding A4 paper in half, then painting the shape of half a butterfly on one side in thick, bright paint, using two colours. Fold the paper again along the centre line while the paint is still wet and press it together. Open it out and talk about how the colours have mixed. Cut out the butterflies and display them.

● Place a Smartie on a wet paper towel and watch the colour appear. Repeat using a Smartie of a different colour. What happens? Why? A similar activity can be carried out using water-based felt-tipped pens.

● Read *Have You Seen the Crocodile?* by Colin West (Walker Books) and look at the pictures of the colourful parrot. They provide a good example of colour-mixing.

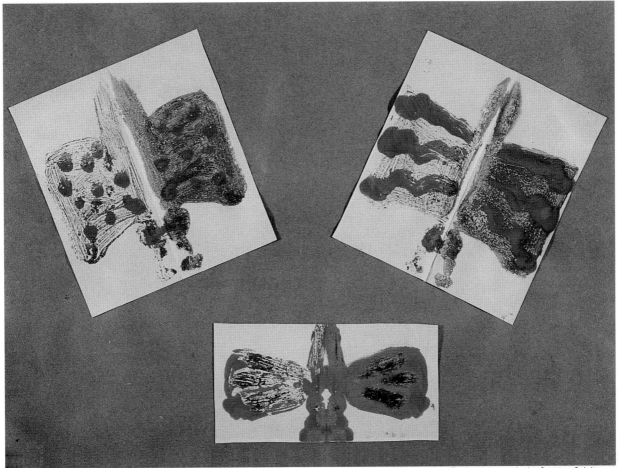

These butterfly prints were made by folding paper in half and painting half a butterfly on one side before refolding.

● Teach the children the song 'Sing a rainbow' in *Apusskidu* (A & C Black).

● Look at examples of brightly coloured clothes and fabrics from Africa and the West Indies. Encourage the children to note and name the different colours used. Ask the children to point out any unusual colours or any interesting combinations.

Involving parents

Ask parents to encourage children in painting and mixing colours. Suggest that they point out and discuss any rainbows they might see,

helping the children to identify and name the colours. Ask them to point out other examples of rainbow-like effects, such as you find in washing-up liquid bubbles or in light shining through textured glass.

Example

Boats in Collioure
by André Derain

In this painting Derain dabs blocks of different colours close to each other to create the impression of mixed colour. The blues and greens representing the sea are particularly effective.

Tone (black and white)

Intended learning

To introduce the children to tone through exploring black and white; to recognise light and dark things; to discuss the contrast between light and dark; to understand the concept of light and dark.

Responding to: *Little Penguin* by Patrick Benson (Walker Books)

Pip is a little penguin busy exploring the world around her. This book follows her day as she slides in the snow, skates on the ice and swims with her whale friend. Pip's black and white colouring and her snowy Antarctic environment provide a good illustration of the contrast of black and white.

Key vocabulary

light, dark, black, white, same, different

The activity

You will need:

a black and white soft toy, a copy of *Little Penguin* by Patrick Benson, yoghurt pots, glue, black fabric, white fabric, black paper, white paper, cotton wool or polystyrene balls, Plasticine, matchsticks, polystyrene blocks, paint, papier mâché, polystyrene scraps.

Points for discussion

Show the children a black and white toy animal, such as a panda. Which part is black? Which part is white? What is the colour of the ears? Is the tail black? Talk about any other black and white animals the children may have seen.

Cats, zebras and cows were among the black and white animals the children chose to paint.

After the discussion

● Read *Little Penguin* together, talking about the illustrations and how Pip stands out against the white snow and ice. Emphasise the contrast in the penguins' colouring.

● Help the children to make their own penguins. Use yoghurt pots covered in black fabric or paper for the body. Then glue on white fabric or paper for the breast, black paper wing shapes, cotton wool or polystyrene balls for the head, Plasticine feet, matchstick legs, and paper eyes and beak.

Display the penguins together against icebergs made from paper and polystyrene blocks. The children could also paint a pool, and make some rocks from papier mâché for their penguins to sit on. Alternatively, they could use polystyrene scraps to represent snow.

Using polystyrene scraps to create a snowstorm for the children's penguin display

17

Assessment

● Can the children distinguish between black and white?

● Can they identify light and dark?

● Can they sort objects into sets of black and sets of white?

● Can they select and use correctly black and white to represent a given object?

Evidence of the children's learning

There was a lot of excitement when the penguins were being made and heated discussions as to whether the heads should be black or white. The children were very keen to find pictures of real penguins to look at and discuss. Some of the children could remember having seen penguins at the zoo, and this led on to discussions of other black and white animals they had seen. When the display was complete, the children enjoyed playing imaginative games with the penguins and the snowscape.

Differentiating the activity

● Most children should be able to recognise black and white but some might need reinforcement. Provide a variety of sorting activities, for example sorting black and white soft toys, articles of clothing, etc., and encourage observation and discussion.

● More able children should be able to use scraper boards to create their own designs.

● Encourage the use of pen and ink, and charcoal for observational drawings.

Extension activities

● Cut or tear snowflakes from small squares or circles of white paper. The finished snowflakes can be mounted on black sugar paper.

● Look together at newspapers and magazines, then tear or cut out some black and white shapes. Use them to make a random collage.

● Try using white chalk on black paper and black crayon on white paper.

● Talk about where black and white occur in the environment, then go on a discovery walk. Discuss any black and white objects you see.

● Make a collection of found objects in black, such as lids, plastic tubes, wool, twine, buttons, spills, buckles, etc., to glue onto white card to depict an imaginary black and white machine.

● Use black wax crayons on white paper to make rubbings of various textured items.

● Place doilies on black paper then paint over them with white paint mixed with glitter. Remove the doilies carefully to reveal snowflake patterns.

● Make a 'black and white' display table. Prepare a chart with two columns headed 'black' and 'white'. Encourage the children to write the names of the objects into the appropriate columns.

● Make clay beads in an assortment of shapes, then paint them black and white. Thread them on string to create patterns, and make them into bracelets or necklaces to give as gifts.

● Create a black and white puppet theatre. Draw shapes representing nursery rhyme characters using black pen on white paper. Glue them onto black card and attach them to pieces of dowelling to make stick puppets. Let the children work in pairs to devise and perform their own nursery rhyme puppet performances.

More able children could make silhouette shapes out of black sugar paper to use as shadow puppets.

Involving parents

Invite parents to find black and white pictures in magazines and papers for school use. They could also collect black and white objects, as well as helping their children to observe the black and white things around the home. Ask them to make a collection of black and white photographs from family albums. Encourage grandparents to talk about the changes in photography from black and white to colour.

Example

Current
by Bridget Riley

Riley's work often involves the stark contrast between black and white, sometimes creating optical illusions. *Current* shows a simple wave pattern in black and white.

Tone (shade)

Intended learning

To notice different shades within one colour; to be able to order shades from lightest to darkest; to understand that by adding white, colours can be lightened; to experiment with colours to create new shades.

Responding to: *I Know Who Jesus Is* by Helen Caswell (The Lutterworth Press)

'Lots of times I wonder about Jesus, and how he lived on earth a long time ago. I wish I could have been there.' The stories of Jesus are often depicted in stained glass windows, like the one at the beginning of this book. Stained glass provides a good opportunity for exploration of shades of colour. This activity could be used as part of a Christmas theme.

Key vocabulary

shade, change, light, lighter, lightest, dark, darker, darkest

The activity

You will need:

a collection of objects in different shades of red, paint colour charts, paint, a copy of *I Know Who Jesus Is* by Helen Caswell, A4 paper, black pen, scissors, card.

Points for discussion

● Show the children the collection of red objects and select one as an example of middle of the range, one as light and one as dark. Ask them if they can order the rest of the objects from light to dark.

● Look at the paint colour charts together. How many different shades of the same colour can they see? Explain how adding white changes a colour and demonstrate by mixing white paint with other colours. Ask the children what has happened to the original colours.

After the discussion

● If possible, before the activity, take the children to see some examples of stained glass windows. Encourage them to try to identify as many shades of colour as they can.

● Share the book *I Know Who Jesus Is* together. Draw the children's attention to the stained glass window picture and talk about how it contains different shades of the same colour. Talk about how some stained glass windows do not show pictures but are made up of patterns.

● Explain that the children are going to make their own stained glass windows.

Ask the children each to fold a sheet of A4 paper into four, then let them make two more folds in any direction. Ask the children each to choose a primary colour.

Let them unfold the paper then get them to fill one of the sections on the sheet with paint of their chosen colour. Then ask them to add a little bit of white to the paint and fill in another section of the paper.

Stained glass window paintings can be used to explore the various possible shades of one colour. In this example, four different paintings were arranged together to make a display.

Repeat, adding a little more white paint each time, until all the sections are filled. What do they notice? When the sheets of paper are dry, help them to separate the sections from each other using thick lines drawn with a black pen.

● For a Christmas theme, card could be folded in half and pre-cut to a church window shape, then black lines drawn on to make random divisions. The children could then be asked to paint in the divisions using different shades of the same colour in the same way as before, to make Christmas cards.

Assessment

● Can the children sort shades of one colour into light and dark?

● Can the children order shades from light to dark, and dark to light?

● Can they make shades of one colour?

● Can they use shades of one colour to create an effect?

Evidence of the children's learning

Looking at paint colour charts provoked much discussion. Some colours were difficult to categorise, such as turquoise, which some children wanted to call blue and others green. The children were surprised and intrigued at how many variations in colour there were. The children were fascinated with the effects of adding white to other colours. 'White is a magic colour,' said Declan on experimenting with all the primary colours. 'Look what it does to red! I've now got pink.'

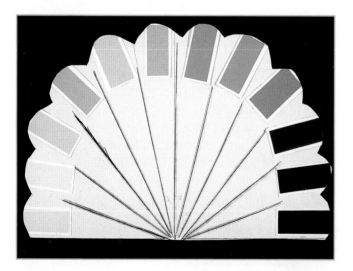

Differentiating the activity

● Some children will need experience of many preliminary activities to help them recognise that there are different shades within one colour. Mix up paint colour charts and encourage children to sort the colours into sets of shades, or sort a collection of buttons into colours before threading sets of shades from light to dark and dark to light.

● Make a playing card game to reinforce the concept of shade. You will need to prepare cards painted on one side in shades red, blue, yellow, orange, purple and green. Make two cards of each colour (for example, pale blue and royal blue). To play the game, place all the cards face downwards so the painted side cannot be seen. Let the children take it in turns to pick up two cards. If the cards are different shades of the same colour, the child may keep them. If they are shades of different colours, they must replace them. Continue until all the cards have been used up. The child with the most pairs of cards at the end is the winner.

Extension activities

● To decorate the classroom for Christmas, draw pointed window outlines on the window panes using a black felt-tipped pen. Make random divisions as before, and get the children to paint the segments different shades of the same colour.

● Look at the shades of children's hair and talk about the differences. Challenge the children to try to match a partner's hair colour by mixing paints. Let them paint a card circle once they have achieved a satisfactory shade, then draw their friend's face on a smaller circle of card and glue it onto the larger circle. Make a display by grouping the faces together according to hair shade.

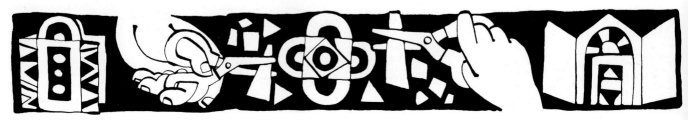

Involving parents

Ask the parents to reinforce the work on shade by collecting colour charts from DIY shops, and by collecting buttons, scrap materials, etc., for the children to bring in to school.

Example

Morning Sunshine
by Rowland Hilder

This painting clearly demonstrates Rowland Hilder's use of tone. He moves from light to dark tones of browns and greens throughout the countryside scene. There is a definite influence of Constable in the painting.

wind round strips of crêpe paper

● Make Christmas lanterns by cutting a piece of black sugar paper 30 × 15 cm. Fold a 2 cm strip at the end, then fold the remainder into four panels. Draw circles, squares, triangles and rectangles in the panels and cut them out. Join the two ends together by applying glue to the end strip, then glue tissue paper in various shades of the same colour over the shapes from the inside. Attach a handle cut from black sugar paper.

● Make party hats from strips of card measuring 5 × 50 cm. Wind thin strips of crêpe paper in white, pink, red and maroon around the strips, creating a range of shades. Join the ends together and decorate the hat with beads. Have a 'Shade Party' with food and drink coloured in different shades of the same colour. Check first that none of the children are allergic to food colouring.

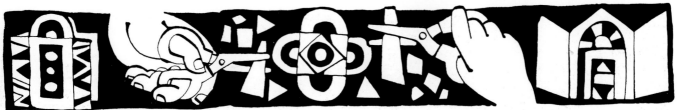

Experiencing patterns

Intended learning

For the children to know what a pattern is and to recognise similarities and differences; to recognise patterns occurring in the natural world; to recognise man-made patterns; to talk about patterns; to understand that there is a range of patterns.

Responding to: *Elmer on Stilts* by David McKee (Red Fox)

'It wasn't long before the elephants were walking on stilts leaving a trail of prints pointing away from them.' Elmer's coat is a fine example of a random pattern, in contrast to the repeated pattern made by the trail of stilts.

Key vocabulary

pattern, same, different, repeat, large, small, again

The activity

You will need:

examples of patterns in wallpaper, fabric, mosaics, crockery, etc., a copy of *Elmer on Stilts* by David McKee, skittles, balls, hoops, beanbags, ropes, quoits, leaves, building blocks, spills, shells, beakers, drawing and painting equipment, card, scissors, glue, pattern-making equipment as suggested by the children (for example, string, matchsticks, seeds, pasta, polystyrene flakes, paper strips).

Points for discussion

● Talk about how a pattern is made. What is a pattern? Then look at examples. Does the pattern repeat? How?

● Invite the children to go on a discovery walk and see how many patterns they can find outside. Look for snail shells, spiders' webs, footprints, tyre tracks, brick walls, wire netting, railings and flower patterns.

● See how many patterns can be found in the classroom on floors, book jackets, clothing, windows, radiators, etc.

After the discussion

● Read *Elmer on Stilts* together. Help the children to recognise that Elmer's patchwork coat is a random pattern (i.e. the basic motif of the coloured patches occurs randomly). As you share the illustrations, encourage the children to look for other examples of pattern, leading them to be able to differentiate between random and regular patterns. (The line of stilt prints is a repeated pattern in that the basic motif is repeated at regular intervals.)

● Invite the children to work in small groups to make repeating patterns in a large space using skittles and balls, hoops and beanbags, ropes and quoits. Encourage them to try out a variety of patterns and to discuss them as they work.

● Allow the children to work individually to make patterns from leaves, building blocks, spills, shells, beakers, etc. Ask them to record their patterns by drawing or painting them.

● Talk about the various nursery rhymes the children know. Explain that they are going to look for as many different patterns around them as possible, both in the classroom and around the grounds, and use them in a nursery rhyme display.

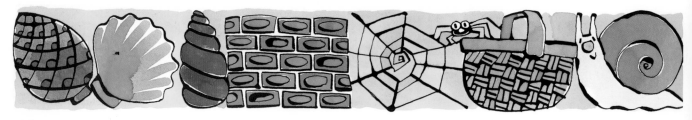

As they find examples of patterns, list them, then discuss how they could be made on the display. Examples could include:

Little Miss Muffet – a spider's web pattern from an assortment of strings;

The old woman in a basket – paper-weaving to make a basket pattern;

Humpty Dumpty – rubbings of toy bricks to make a wall pattern;

Mary Mary – a pattern of sea shells to represent cockle shells.

Encourage each child to make a different nursery rhyme pattern on a sheet of paper. Let the children paint cardboard figures to represent the nursery rhyme characters and help them to cut them out. Paint a background before gluing on the various figures and their associated patterns.

Add a caption for the display, such as 'How many patterns can you see in our nursery rhyme picture?'.

Coloured cotton reels are among many classroom items that can be used to investigate repeating patterns.

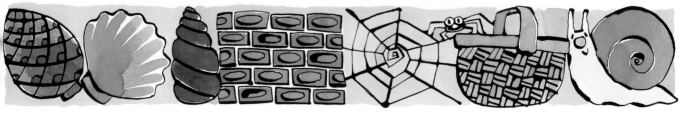

Assessment

● Can the children find patterns in the environment?

● Can the children recognise a man-made pattern?

● Observe the children discussing patterns. Do they use the words 'repeat', 'same as' and 'again'?

● Can they differentiate between a random pattern and a repeat pattern?

Evidence of the children's learning

Some of the children found it difficult to understand the concept of placing two objects in a pattern. Rachel wanted all her skittles to be together but her partner, Fiona, placed the balls and skittles in alternate patterns. One group placed beanbags in hoops while others alternated them. The children were keen to change the apparatus to make different patterns. They were very enthusiastic about finding patterns in the environment and were able to use them as inspiration for their display.

Differentiating the activity

Children who need further practical experience of exploring pattern could be helped by sequencing activities: farm animals could be arranged to represent repeating patterns and coloured cotton reels could be threaded on string. Adhesive shapes could also be used to reinforce the concept of repeating patterns.

Extension activities

● The children could recreate observed patterns by putting shoes on their hands and printing on damp sand in the sand tray; making repeating handprints with paint; using matchsticks and Plasticine to make birds' footprints; using tyres in puddles in the playground to make tyre tracks; or running the wheels of toy vehicles through a tray of paint, then rolling them over a sheet of paper.

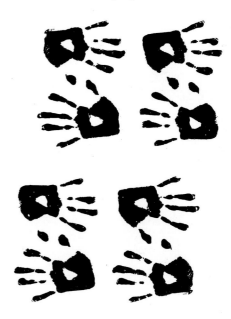

● Look at examples of Roman mosaic patterns in books, postcards or photographs.

● Investigate face and body painting from different cultures (for example, mehndi patterns from North Africa or Maori tattoos from New Zealand).

● Use polystyrene packaging flakes, seeds or pasta to make necklaces or collage patterns.

● Look at examples of English china (Denby, Coalport, Crown Derby, Mason, etc.) and see what kinds of patterns are used. Then let the children make their own patterns using paint mixed with PVA glue on paper plates.

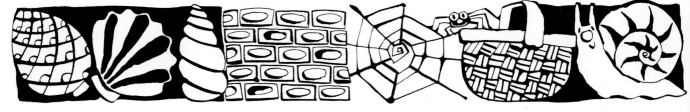

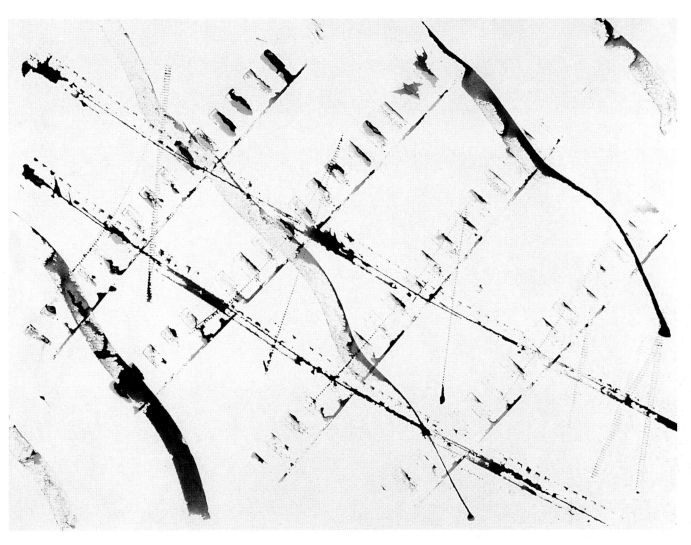

The wheels of toy vehicles were used to make this pattern.

Involving parents

Invite the parents to contribute holiday souvenirs and pictures that demonstrate definite patterns (mosaics, pottery, fabrics, ties, scarves, etc.) and use these for a classroom display on patterns. Ask parents to encourage their children to look out for examples of patterns in the environment.

Example

The funerary mask of Tutankhamun

There are many examples of pattern to be seen on this familiar artefact. The children can identify circles, triangles, squares and repeated colours.

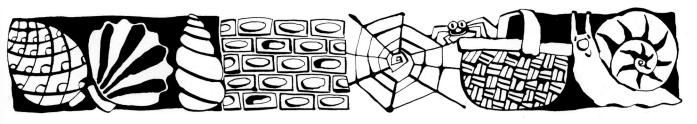

Pattern-making

Intended learning

To build on the children's experience of pattern; to use examples from the environment to stimulate pattern-making; to create designs using a range of techniques.

Responding to: *The Town Mouse and the Country Mouse* (traditional story)

Country Mouse lives in a tree, while Town Mouse lives in a town house. In this activity, children create a class book using different patterns to bring out the extreme contrasts in the way the two mice live.

Key vocabulary

pattern, repeat, print, stamp, random, dots, lines, design

The activity

You will need:

painting and drawing equipment, paper, patterned materials (dress fabrics, wallpaper, carpets, etc.), sponge shapes, *The Town Mouse and the Country Mouse* (many versions available – the one published by Ladybird is a good example), natural materials (leaves, sticks, shells, etc.), junk materials (lids, cotton reels, etc.), card, glue.

Points for discussion

● Ask the children to draw a pattern, then discuss the results. (Some children will have drawn repeating patterns where the motif is repeated at regular intervals, while others will have drawn random patterns where the motif is used irregularly at random.) Talk about whether this is a repeating pattern and why.

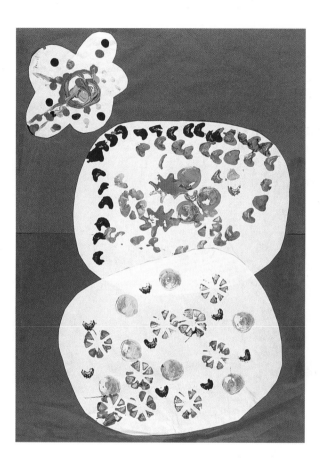

● Show the children examples of patterned materials and encourage them to make comparisons with their own patterns. Talk about how random and repeat patterns differ.

● Help the children to sort random and repeat patterns from your collection of sample materials. Talk about how they might use observed patterns (environmental or man-made) in their own designs.

After the discussion

● Give the children plenty of opportunity to create both random and repeat patterns using fingers and sponge shapes dipped in paint. Then let them try using bright paint and thick brushes to produce dot and line patterns.

● Read *The Town Mouse and the Country Mouse* together, then discuss how you might make a class book of it, incorporating plenty of different types of patterns.

For the cover you might use finger-printing on card in brown, green and yellow paint to create a cornfield background, with pictures of the two mice stuck on.

To make the mice for the cover and the inside pages, give each of the children a piece of card and ask them to draw and cut out a mouse shape. Suggest that they decorate the mice by printing or sticking random patterns on the Country Mouse and repeat patterns on the Town Mouse.

Inside the book, the home of the Country Mouse could be depicted using a collage of natural materials such as leaves, sticks, stones, and so on, in random patterns. The home of the Town Mouse could be made by printing with cotton reels, lids, pots and so on in more regular patterns. On the final pages, include some of the children's own writing decorated with repeat border patterns.

The story of *The Town Mouse and the Country Mouse* was made into a class book full of different sorts of patterns.

Assessment

● Can the children make a random pattern?

● Can the children make a repeated pattern?

● Can the children continue a repeated pattern?

● Can the children use pattern effectively?

● Are the children able to create an original pattern?

Evidence of the children's learning

The children who had experienced both town and country life had a wider experience of environmental patterns and so were able to compare them and talk about them more easily. They readily shared their ideas with their friends. Some children made slow progress from random pattern-making to repeat pattern-making but all were enthusiastic in their approach.

Differentiating the activity

Random patterns will be easy for most children to make. However, repeated patterns may cause more difficulty, and plenty of practice may be required. Sticky-backed paper shapes and stick-on felt shapes can be used to reinforce the concept. Allow children to experiment with positioning the same basic motif both at regular intervals and at random.

Extension activities

● Ask the children to work in pairs to create sequenced patterns, taking turns to print.

● Try using grained wood blocks and paint to make patterns. These could be used for depicting doors, windows, bricks and tiles in displays.

● Encourage the children to make decorative patterned borders when they practise their handwriting.

● Collect a variety of shells for use in pattern-making. Try printing with them into Plasticine.

● Make seasonal greetings cards by printing with repeating patterns. These could include pictures of candles for Divali, flowers for Mother's Day, stars for Christmas and eggs for Easter.

● Use the computer to create number, letter or graphic patterns.

● Provide the children with the beginning of a pattern photocopied onto an A4 sheet of paper, and ask them to complete it, using crayons, paints or felt-tipped pens.

● Try printing with fruit and vegetables. Encourage the children to think of different ways to cut them and to look closely at the patterns made by the seeds in tomatoes, cucumbers, etc.

Involving parents

Ask the parents to set aside objects that might be used for pattern-making and to encourage their children to experiment with different kinds of pattern. Unwanted rolls of wallpaper and pieces of patterned fabric could be collected for class use.

Example

Wallpaper and textile designs
by William Morris

William Morris's work often featured motifs from nature, such as flowers, leaves, fruit and birds. Children will enjoy identifying the various objects in his wallpaper and textile designs and seeing how they are used to make up repeating patterns.

Spatial awareness (2D)

Intended learning

To encourage children to make the best use of the space available in their work; to think about composition when making a picture.

Responding to: familiar rhymes and poems

Familiar rhymes are a useful starting point for exploration of spatial awareness in pictures. Because the children will be familiar with the content of the rhymes, more concentration can be given to placing the objects in space when depicting them in their pictures.

Key vocabulary

space, move, nearer, higher, lower, up, down, side, top, bottom

The activity

You will need:

examples of the children's own pictures, a book or tape of rhymes, black paper, white chalk, paint, paper, scissors, PVA glue, stick-on felt animals and boards, plastic fork or wide-toothed comb, fish templates, textured foil, string, cold clay, blunt modelling tools, varnish.

Points for discussion

● Look at the children's pictures and talk about how they have used space. Ask the children questions about the use of space, bearing in mind the sensitivities of the children whose work is being discussed. Is the tree in the best place? Might it look better touching the ground? Are the flowers the right size? Should they be smaller than the tree? Where would be the best place for the bird? Would you move anything?

● Build the children's confidence by pointing out good examples of spatial awareness. (See how Luke's house is *much bigger* than his car. Tarvinder's mummy is sitting *on* the chair.)

After the discussion

Say or sing together some familiar rhymes, then organise the class into groups to try out some related activities involving careful use of space. The following rhymes offer just a few examples of how spatial awareness can be explored. Encourage the children to think of their own favourite poems and rhymes.

● For *Five Fat Sausages* give each child a black paper cut-out pan and a piece of white chalk. Then ask them to draw five sausages in the pan, leaving a space between each one. Discuss the results.

● Make a group picture for *Incy Wincy Spider*. Small groups could be invited to paint and cut out the spout, large raindrops, sun, the spider and the web. Then the whole class could discuss where everything should go. Stress the importance of moving things around to find the best arrangement before sticking all the items in place.

● Use the stick-on felt animals and boards to depict *Old Macdonald's Farm*. Encourage the children to work in pairs to place the animals on the board in response to the song. Look at the boards together. Have the children used the space well?

● For *One, Two, Three, Four, Five* make a large frieze together. Begin by getting the children to paint the background with blue-green paint mixed with PVA. Show them how they can make a rippled effect by dragging a plastic fork or wide-toothed comb across the painted surface. Next let them draw round fish templates on textured foil. Cut out five fish shapes and let the children stick them onto the water, making sure they use all the space. Finally let them paint an angler dangling a fishing line made from string in the water.

● For *The House that Jack Built* let each child makes a cold clay tile measuring 15 × 15 cm. Decide with the children who is going to illustrate which part of the rhyme (mouse, cat, dog, etc.), then let them use a blunt tool to draw the house, Jack and their chosen animal, using the whole of the tile. Paint and varnish the tiles, and display them in sequence.

The child who painted this picture carefully positioned Humpty Dumpty in front of the wall and below the sun.

Assessment

● Can the children talk about the position of the objects in a picture?

● Can the children suggest alternative placings for objects within their pictures?

● Can children use space to the best advantage?

Differentiating the activity

● The use of space can be very difficult for children to understand. Continue using more familiar rhymes to illustrate the idea. For *The Wheels on the Bus*, get the children to add wheels to an outline of a bus. For *I'm a Little Teapot*, a lid, handle and spout could be used for placing activities.

Left: this work by a three-year old already shows a basic under-standing of spatial relationships.

Right: these drawings by slightly older children show a more sophisti-cated awareness.

Evidence of the children's learning

Many children found it hard to understand how their own placing of objects might be arranged in a more realistic way ('Why aren't my little men all right at the bottom of the page?'). It had to be carefully explained that a lot of space had been left empty and that the people in their pictures were so important that they needed to be seen clearly.

● Give as many varied opportunities as possible for children to get used to using space well, for example with chalk on the blackboard and with paint on paper. Before they start painting or drawing, remind them to try to use the whole of the sheet of paper. Using stick-on felt shapes which the children can reposition easily, can help to build up confidence and spatial awareness.

Extension activities

● Invite the children to work in pairs to make a class rhyme frieze. Each pair should take a different rhyme, then draw, paint or colour the top half of a sheet of A4 paper with a representative picture, making good use of the space. On the bottom half of the sheet, help the children to write out the words of the rhyme.

● Each child could make an individual rhyme book, choosing their favourite rhyme for the cover and depicting it with a paper collage using foil, tissue, wallpaper, magazines, newspaper, etc. Encourage them to think carefully about placing the collage materials, rearranging them if necessary, before finally sticking them in place.

Involving parents

Invite parents to prepare for the activity by sharing favourite rhymes and songs with their children, then drawing or painting them together. Ask them to stress position words to encourage the children's spatial awareness (the sausages are *in* the pan, Humpty is *on* the wall, the cow jumped *over* the moon).

Example

Sunflowers
by Vincent van Gogh

Sunflowers provides an excellent model of how to make the best use of available space. Children could be asked to paint a similar picture, with large, cheerful flowers filling their paper.

Spatial awareness (3D)

Intended learning

To move the children forward from an understanding of two- to three-dimensional art; to experience spatial awareness through three-dimensional art; to develop an understanding of three dimensions; for the children to create their own three-dimensional work.

Responding to: *Thomas and the Lost Cat* by Christopher Awdry and Ken Stott (Heinemann)

When a cat escapes from Thomas's train, his driver, guard and all the passengers help to find him. Thomas has been a children's favourite for many years and the television series has enhanced his popularity. Making a train from cardboard boxes and creating games in and around it gives real meaning to three-dimensional work.

Key vocabulary

depth, flat, make, space, front, behind, around, inside, outside, through

The activity

You will need:

an assortment of small boxes and containers, a copy of *Thomas and the Lost Cat* by Christopher Awdry and Ken Stott, paper, large and strong cardboard boxes, adhesive tape, glue, scissors, kitchen paper, paints, cardboard, inner tube from a roll of carpet, cardboard tubes, dressing-up clothes such as a train-driver's hat and jacket.

Points for discussion

● Talk about how objects have depth. Show the children the collection of containers. Encourage them to handle and describe them.

● Show the children a sheet of paper and encourage them to compare it with the containers. Can they describe the difference between them?

● Talk about how the containers might be put together to make an interesting arrangement. Encourage free experimentation by placing several containers together, on top of each other, side by side, behind each other, etc.

After the discussion

● Read *Thomas and the Lost Cat* together. Talk about Thomas's shape.

● Show the children the large boxes and invite them to climb on, walk through and sit in them. Allow them to handle the boxes and move them around on the floor. Ask them how they might arrange the boxes to make a train like Thomas.

● Explain that they are going to make their own train. Fasten together a range of cardboard boxes with adhesive tape to form the basic train shape, cutting the sides away as necessary. Cover them with kitchen paper, and paint them in blue, red, yellow and black. Stick on a large circle of card at the front of the train and paint on Thomas's characteristic smiling face.

The 'Fat Controller' and the station cat could be made from cardboard and stood against a painted station backdrop. Make a signal from strips of cardboard and cardboard tubes.

Provide suitable dressing-up clothes and allow the children plenty of time for imaginative play in Thomas, reinforcing the idea that they have created a piece of three-dimensional art.

The children loved playing in Thomas as much as they enjoyed creating him.

Assessment

● Can the children differentiate between two and three dimensions using the word 'depth'?

● Can the children create meaningful three-dimensional models?

● Do the children fully understand the difficult concept of three dimensions?

Evidence of the children's learning

The children's imaginations were well stimulated in this three-dimensional activity, and they had great fun. Everyone wanted to participate and they positioned their boxes enthusiastically. The children loved Thomas so much that a timer had to be used to restrict playing time. It was a tremendous success and brought the stories to life for the children, as well as enhancing their appreciation of spatial relationships.

Differentiating the activity

Making vehicles from construction kit materials such as LEGO is a useful experience for all children in order to reinforce the concept of three-dimensional art. Many children will not wholly understand the concept, so it is important to give plenty of opportunities to practise and discuss.

Extension activities

● Create a three-dimensional underwater scene inside an old fish tank. Help the children to paint reeds, plants, coral and seaweed on the inside of three sides of the tank using ready-mixed paint. Cover the base of the tank with painted stones, shells and wood.

Let the children make fish from card and small boxes and decorate them with fluorescent paint. Stretch thread across the top of the tank and fasten it in place with adhesive tape, then use it to suspend the fish.

● Make a three-dimensional moonscape display by first covering a display table with silver foil. Then cut polystyrene to represet craters and rocks and stick it onto the foil. Make two moonmobiles by covering an old football with paper and paste, then cutting it in half. Paint each half with silver paint and add cardboard wheels. Place the moonmobiles on the display. The children could add play people to represent astronauts. Finally, let the children create rockets from plastic bottles covered in foil, with cardboard fins either covered in foil or painted with metallic paint. These could be suspended from the ceiling above the display.

● Read *The Dinosaur's Egg* by Christina M. Butler and Val Biro (Simon and Schuster Young Books), then encourage the children to make their own dinosaur cave and rocky landscape. Use large cardboard boxes fastened together with adhesive tape, then covered with kitchen paper and painted brown and grey shades. Cut a giant dinosaur from corrugated card. Stick on lids, buttons etc., to add features before painting it. Use inflated balloons covered in strips of papier mâché to represent dinosaur eggs and place them in the cave. Encourage free play in and around the dinosaur's cave.

● Children with developed cutting skills could make a Mother's Day card by layering flowers cut from wrapping paper, stuck together at the centre with double-sided sticky tape to give a three-dimensional effect. The paper should have a bold design.

● Provide dried flowers, acorns, twigs, small cones and beech nuts for the children to use to decorate a card frame for a school photograph.

Involving parents

Ask for parents' help in collecting boxes, tubes, yoghurt pots, packaging, stones, shells, etc., which can be used for three-dimensional modelling within the classroom and at home.

Example

Interwoven Circle
by Andy Goldsworthy

This sculpture of woven bamboo was created in 1987 and is a kind of extraordinary basket work. It shows how straight lines can be used to form a three-dimensional effect.

Experiencing texture

Intended learning

To encourage the children to feel the quality of objects and materials through first-hand experience; to help the children to notice differences in how things feel; to discuss with the children the qualities of different textures.

Responding to: *The Circus* by Brian Wildsmith (OUP)

The circus is in town! This picture book, with its circus theme, can inspire children to experiment with all sorts of textures.

Key vocabulary

touch, feel, thick, thin, hard, soft, rough, smooth, furry, fluffy, coarse

The activity

You will need:

a 'feely bag' containing a range of textured objects (a sponge ball, a wooden brick, plastic lids, sandpaper, a fur-covered toy, etc.) and natural materials (a fir cone, a stone, feathers, leaves, etc.). You will also need a selection of fabrics and paper with different textures, sorting boxes, a copy of *The Circus* by Brian Wildsmith, card, glue, scissors, backing paper.

Points for discussion

● Talk about how various items feel. Prepare the 'feely bag', then ask the children to take turns to select an object, feel it in the bag and describe it to the rest of the group. Allow the other children to try to guess what the object is. Encourage the use of appropriate 'texture' vocabulary.

● Discuss how there can be different textures within one room. Invite the children to bring contrasting items with various textures from their bedrooms at home, such as a brush, comb, slippers, nightwear, rug, toy box, etc. Make a display of all the items, and allow opportunities for everyone to touch and talk about the textures.

After the discussion

● Take the children on a discovery walk around the school grounds or in a local park to pick up leaves, stones, conkers, acorns, bark, feathers and twigs. Back in the classroom, ask the children to sort the items into sets of rough and smooth. Then encourage them to look around the classroom for things which feel hard and soft and sort them into sets.

● Then fill a box with a selection of fabrics with different textures, such as silk, hessian, suede, felt, cotton, wool, nylon, carpet, oil cloth and kitchen cloths. Ask the children to sort these into new sets of rough and smooth.

● Look at and talk about *The Circus* by Brian Wildsmith. Refer particularly to the page entitled 'The Circus Comes to Town'.

● Divide the children into three groups, and explain that they are going to produce pictures of performers, caravans and animals respectively for a circus display.

Give each group a range of materials (including the natural materials they found earlier, the fabrics and a selection of textured papers). Explain that each child is to make a cut-out shape of a character or an animal from the story and is to decorate their shape by sticking on appropriate textured materials. Allow the children freedom of choice to select suitable materials as they decorate their characters, caravans or creatures.

With all the children, agree on a suitable arrangement of the figures, then attach them to backing paper to make a circus caravan wall picture.

Fur fabric, cotton, cardboard and foil were just some of the different textures used to create this circus frieze.

Assessment

● Can the children feel the differences between the various textures?

● Can the children find objects of a similar texture and a different texture?

● Can the children use appropriate vocabulary to describe texture?

Evidence of the children's learning

The children had to make a number of choices. They began by sorting the various fabrics into rough and smooth sets. The caravan group then decided that although they liked the soft fluffy materials, they would be unsuitable for what they were doing, and chose smooth shiny materials. The animal-makers had lots of decisions to make. ('My tiger needs a smooth coat, but the elephant needs a rough one. What shall we use for the bear?') The children depicting the people were lucky, as they found that they could use any of the materials effectively for their characters' costumes.

Differentiating the activity

● Children are naturally drawn towards exploring by sense of touch and it is encouraged from a very early age through baby books and toys of differing textures. Children should have no problem recognising textures but they may need many opportunities to use relevant vocabulary. Encourage the children to describe the fabrics as they handle them. Use sand and water play areas as starting points for discussion, by looking at the differences between textures of wet and dry sand.

● The children could also play 'What's in the box?'. Fill three identical boxes with different substances, such as pasta, torn newspaper and sand. Place a large piece of cloth over each of the boxes so that the children cannot see what is in them. Invite a child to feel inside a box and describe what they can feel before guessing what the contents might be. Encourage the use of at least two adjectives to describe the feeling quality.

Extension activities

● Collect a range of different textures (for example, foil, tissue, cellophane, clingfilm, newspaper, cardboard, sandpaper) and display them as a 'texture wheel'. Invite the children to take turns at feeling the wheel and describing the different textures.

● Play 'Who wears what?'. Dress three children in jackets made from different materials, such as leather, wool and cotton. Blindfold another child and ask them to feel the materials. Can the child guess which child is which?

● Create a game to help differentiate between hard/soft and rough/smooth. Put a range of textured objects and fabrics into bags. Ask the group to stand in a line and appoint a leader. Let the leader call out, 'Find a hard/soft/rough/smooth object and bring it to me,' and the rest of the group should take turns to retrieve the appropriately textured article.

● Make texture cards by covering postcards with textured material. Use these to encourage vocabulary development. Some children who find word associations easy could work in pairs to see how many words they can think of to describe a particular texture.

This texture wheel was made from a variety of materials, including fur fabric, bubble wrap and tissue paper.

Involving parents

Ask the parents to provide a range of textures, including mud and sawdust, for home exploration. Invite parents to collect textured materials for use in the classroom, and send home a letter asking them to allow their child to bring in an object from their bedroom. Encourage the early use of touch and feel toys.

Example

The Bayeux Tapestry

A wide range of texture effects are produced by the use of different stitches in this famous tapestry. There are also potential links with work on history.

Using texture

Intended learning

To understand the range of textures that can be used to effect when creating pictures; to use a range of textures effectively; to be able to discuss their use of textures; to extend texture-related vocabulary.

Responding to: *The Three Little Pigs* (traditional story)

The Three Little Pigs each use different textured materials to build their houses: straw, sticks and bricks. This familiar and well-loved tale makes a good starting point for using different textures.

Key vocabulary

touch, feel, use, same, different, smooth, alike, similar, hard, soft

The activity

You will need:

varied textured materials, a version of *The Three Little Pigs* (an appropriate version is published by Ladybird), cardboard boxes, corrugated card, staple gun, straw, sticks, polystyrene sheets cut into squares or oblongs to represent bricks, glue, clay or Plasticine, A4 card, animal templates, scissors, painting and colouring equipment.

Points for discussion

● Talk about how texture can be used to create interesting effects. Reinforce the ideas previously explored in *Experiencing texture* by getting the children to sort and label different textured items.

● Discuss how the children might use textures in making models and pictures. Ask questions such as, 'What would be a good material to represent bricks in a model of a house?', or 'Would this piece of felt be good for making a picture of a sheep? Why not? What could you use instead?'

After the discussion

● Read the story of *The Three Little Pigs* to the children. Discuss the textures of the materials used for the three houses, then suggest that the children make houses from large cardboard boxes, with roofs made from sheets of corrugated card bent in the middle.

Staple the roofs in position for the children, then let them glue on straw, sticks and polystyrene (to represent bricks) to cover the houses. Then ask the children to make the pigs and wolf from clay or Plasticine. Encourage free play with the wolf, the pigs and their houses.

● To reinforce the concept of texture, give each child a piece of A4 card folded in half. Ask them to draw an animal outline onto one half of the card. Next help the children to make a hole in the centre of the animal outline. Ask them to choose an appropriate textured material for the animal, then to glue a piece of the material inside the folded card, exposing the texture through the hole.

Let the children complete their pictures by colouring and drawing on facial features. Join the cards together to make a touch and feel book. Share the book as a group, discussing the various textures.

Choosing suitable materials to make houses for the Three Little Pigs

Assessment

● Can the children use a range of textures with effect?

● Do the children select appropriately from a range of textures for their work?

● Listen to the children's choice of words as they make their selection. Do they use appropriate vocabulary?

Evidence of the children's learning

The children thoroughly enjoyed the mess involved with this activity and they became competitive in seeing whose house would be finished first. As they talked about their work, they described the straw as scratchy and bendy, the sticks as hard and rough and the polystyrene as both rough and smooth. Making the texture book also provoked a lot of imaginative vocabulary to describe what the various fabrics felt like.

Differentiating the activity

It may be necessary for children who have difficulty in making choices regarding texture to have the choice of materials restricted. Bear in mind that fluffy material will always be a favourite, but will often be inappropriate, so it might be necessary to remove such materials from the selection.

Extension activities

● Make a firework display picture using thick finger paints mixed with PVA on black paper. Decorate it with glitter and ask the children to make a guy made of different textured fabrics to stick on it.

● Introduce the use of different types of shading to represent various textures in observational drawings.

● Increase the amount of materials available and let the children design their own individual textured collages.

● Make weaving frames by giving the children squares of card with parallel lines about 2 cm apart cut into them. Make sure that the cuts end no less than 2 cm from the edge of the card. Provide strips of textured paper to weave in and out to make a texture sampler. Show the children how to secure the ends of the strips with glue.

● Use the paper weaving technique to make baskets of flowers, with decorative gift bows to represent flowers.

● Give small groups of children an assortment of dried pasta or seeds, and ask them to make decorative wall hangings by gluing them to a paper plate then painting it with brightly coloured paint. Alternatively, individual children could be invited to make masks by sticking seeds and pulses onto face shapes cut from card.

● Create texture gardens on a plate, using natural materials, such as moss, stones, flowers, grass and twigs, perhaps adding a mirror to represent a pond.

Paper-weaving was used to make this basket of flowers.

Involving parents

Ask parents to collect a wide variety of textured materials and to become involved in play activities to reinforce the similarities and differences between textures. Parents who enjoy knitting, crochet, lace-making and needlepoint activities could be asked to describe their work to their children and to talk about the various textures.

Example

Oil paintings

Oil paintings have interesting and varied textures but this cannot be seen in reproductions. The children need to be able to see real paintings to understand and experience the technique involved. Rather than suggesting any one painting, a visit to your local art gallery is recommended here.

Discovering form

Intended learning

To introduce the children to a range of materials; to use touch to discover the properties of different materials; to explore how materials can change shape.

Responding to: *Honeybee's Busy Day* by Richard Fowler (Doubleday Press)

Honeybee has been busy all day collecting nectar to make into honey. The children's imagination can be stimulated by this story, encouraging them to use their modelling skills to recreate the tiny world of Honeybee and his minibeast friends.

Key vocabulary

squeeze, roll, squash, flatten, coil, stretch, press, change, feel

The activity

You will need:

play dough (1 cup water, 1 cup plain flour, ½ cup salt, 1 tablespoon cooking oil, 2 teaspoons cream of tartar and food colouring all mixed together, warmed in a pan and kneaded until smooth). You will also need a picture of a snail, a selection of modelling tools (for example, blunt sticks, cutters, cotton reels and a rolling pin), Plasticine, clay, a copy of *Honeybee's Busy Day* by Richard Fowler, cress and mustard seeds germinated on a piece of damp flannel or kitchen towel (enough for each child to have a small batch of seedlings).

Points for discussion

● Talk about how play dough changes shape. Give each child a lump of play dough to roll, squeeze, squash and stretch. How many different shapes can be made? Encourage each child to show and discuss what they have made.

● Talk about how play dough can be changed into a specific shape. Look at a picture of the shell of a snail. Talk about how it coils. Can the children make a coil shape? Now can they make a snail shell?

● Next invite the children to use a range of tools to experiment with changing the shape of materials such as Plasticine, play dough or clay. Let the children experiment using different materials and different tools. Encourage them to make lines, holes, dents and patterns.

Rolling, wedging and shaping

After the discussion

● Read *Honeybee's Busy Day*. Talk about what it would be like to be tiny like Honeybee and his friends. What would the world look like?

● Suggest how the children might use clay or Plasticine to model the miniature world of Honeybee. Encourage them to use the modelling tools and the squashing, rolling and coiling techniques to form bees, mushrooms, snails, spiders, ladybirds, flowers, hedgehogs, etc.

When the children have finished modelling their minibeasts and plants, let them arrange their creations among the cress seedlings to recreate a scene from the story. Encourage retelling of the story as they work.

Adding texture with modelling tools

Assessment

● Do the children become involved in changing the form of the materials?

● Can the children use appropriate vocabulary to describe what they are doing?

Evidence of the children's learning

The children quickly became involved in feeling, squeezing and pulling at the materials. Harminda didn't like the feel of the clay because it stuck to his hands, but he enjoyed modelling using the tools. Natalie modelled carefully, using finer detail. Jane's imagination took over; she had to include fairies and in the end made a fairy glen.

Differentiating the activity

Most children will enjoy the activities without realising that they are changing the form of their materials. Children with difficulties will need as many opportunities as possible to experiment with changing form: a mixture of mud and water is an ideal material as it is easily accessible and can be squeezed, poured and made into shapes.

Extension activities

● Challenge the children to explore the form of a shoe box and to find an alternative use. The sides could be broken and the box could be used to make a paper puppet theatre or it could be used as a garage or a pencil box. Several boxes could be combined to make into dolls' houses, animal homes, building blocks, and so on.

● Use flat pieces of paper to make rockets for a mobile. Help the children to make cones from the paper and decorate them appropriately. For example, card fins could be added, windows with astronauts could be painted or stuck on and strips of orange and red crêpe paper could be attached to the ends to look like jets of flame. Display them suspended with thread.

● Model with papier mâché, made by tearing newspaper into strips and mixing it with wallpaper paste. A balloon covered with papier mâché could provide the basis for a Christmas decoration, Cinderella's coach, or homes for imaginary people. Long balloons used in a similar way could be used to model aeroplanes, submarines or sausage dogs. Alternatively the papier mâché could be used for modelling with the hands.

● Experiment in the sand tray with wet and dry sand to create different forms (sandcastles, pies, shapes, tracks, etc.).

● Introduce the children to a new modelling medium by providing them with salt dough. This can be made by blending 2 level cups of plain flour, 1 heaped cup of table salt and 1 tablespoon of wallpaper paste. Pour on 1 cup of lukewarm water and 1 tablespoon of vegetable oil. Knead by hand for 10 to 15 minutes. If the dough is too dry, add a little water. If it is too sticky, add a little more flour.

Use salt dough to make calendar plaques that the children can take home as a Christmas or New Year gift. Let them roll out the dough, cut out an interesting shape with pastry cutters, and then add texture with modelling tools. Help them to make holes at the bottom of the plaque. Let them paint their plaques and, when dry, thread ribbon through the holes to attach a calendar.

● Experiment with the different forms that can be made by using moulds. This could be as simple as making sandcastles using buckets of wet sand or making jelly in moulds for a class party. The children could also be helped to pour melted chocolate into moulds. When the chocolate is set they could wrap it in coloured foil, carefully shaping the foil round the form of the chocolate.

● More dextrous children could be invited to try sewing fabric scraps to make hats and other garments for dolls and teddies. To begin with, use fairly loosely woven fabrics, blunt needles and thick thread.

● Drill holes through conkers, acorns, and so on, and let the children experiment with threading them onto string or thick wool to make snakes, necklaces, puppets, etc.

● Make a biscuit dough from sugar, margarine and flour. Talk about the form of each ingredient and how they change when combined with the others. Let the children experiment with moulding the dough in their hands, rolling it out and cutting out biscuits using shaped cutters. Discuss the different forms made.

● Use a range of construction kit materials, such as LEGO or plastic straws to experiment with making new forms.

Involving parents

Make parents aware of the many possibilities for talking with their children about how things change their form. Ask them to encourage free play at home with boxes, Plasticine, play dough, etc.

Example

Various sculptures
by Elisabeth Frink

Elisabeth Frink's many animal sculptures, such as the *Horse* series or *Leonardo's Dog*, have an immediate appeal for children, while their interesting shapes and textures make them a useful aid to the exploration of form.

Changing the form

Intended learning

To understand how materials can be used in various ways; to make choices about suitable materials and to be able to talk about them; to develop techniques to change the form of materials; to create artefacts and pictures from observation and imagination and to discuss the outcome.

> Responding to: the song 'The Music Man' in *Okki-tokki-unga* (A & C Black)
>
> > I am a music man
> > I come from far away
> > And I can play...
>
> This familiar song can be adapted to introduce a range of musical instruments, which the children can then make from everyday objects.

Key vocabulary

join, match, model, change, choose, shape, make, create, best, wrong

The activity

You will need:

corrugated paper, clay, a copy of the song 'The Music Man', a large card tube (such as the inner tube from a roll of carpet), smaller card tubes (such as inner tubes from rolls of tin foil), empty drinks cans, an old football, a paper plate, painting equipment, glue, wool, strong adhesive tape, unwanted clothing (a hat, a colourful shirt and trousers or thick, coloured

tights would be ideal), small hooks, needle and thread, found materials to make musical instruments (small plastic bottles, dowelling and rice for maracas; egg box, string and stick for a guiro; tissue box and rubber bands for a kalimba; bells and string; large tins and bottle tops), paper, scissors, adhesive tape, string.

Points for discussion

● Talk about how one material is more appropriate for a particular task than another.

● Show the children two contrasting materials, such as clay and corrugated paper. Which material would be best for making a teapot? Why? Lead the children to understand that the paper would go soggy when water was put in it.

● Ask the children to find other materials for making a teapot. Discuss their suitability, then ask them to make two sets – suitable and unsuitable. How would the children change the form of the material to make a teapot? If possible, let them try their ideas out.

After the discussion

● Sing the song 'The Music Man' then explain that the children are going to make their own model of the Music Man and a range of musical instruments for him to carry.

● First decide how to make the figure of the Music Man. Encourage the children to make choices as to the most appropriate materials to use for a body (card tube from carpet roll), arms and legs (inner tubes from roll of tin foil), feet (drinks cans) and head (football). Help the children to join them together with strong adhesive tape. Make a face by sticking on a paper plate, add appropriate features, then glue on wool for hair. Dress the Music Man in brightly coloured clothes. Sew on small hooks on which to hang instruments.

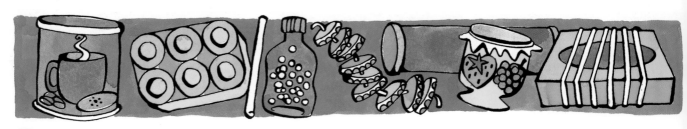

Talk about the instruments the Music Man might carry and how the children might make them. Where appropriate, talk about the countries and cultures the instruments are from.

To make Latin American maracas, decorate small plastic bottles and fill them with rice before inserting a piece of dowelling into the neck and sealing it tightly with adhesive tape.

To make a Mexican guiro (scraper), paint cardboard egg boxes and attach a stick with a length of string. Show the children how to make a noise by scraping the stick along the underside of the box.

To make an African kalimba, stretch rubber bands of different thickness widthways across a decorated tissue box and let the children pluck the 'strings' across the hole.

Other instruments could include bells suspended on strings; drums made from catering size coffee tins or biscuit tins, covered and decorated; jingles from bottle tops with holes punched in them, joined together with string and attached to a stick.

Attach a string loop to each of the instruments and hang them from the hooks on the Music Man's clothing.

All sorts of materials were used to make drums, shakers and other instruments for the Music Man to carry and for the children to play.

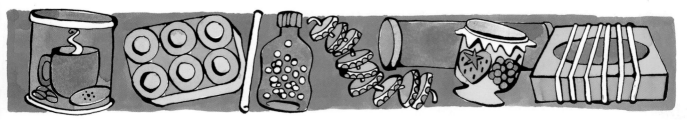

Assessment

● Do the children recognise that there are appropriate materials for particular purposes?

● Can the children make suitable choices of materials?

● Can they give reasons for their choices?

● Do they use materials well?

● What do they make?

Evidence of the children's learning

Several children knew the song already but were excited to see the form of the Music Man take shape. His clothes and instruments provoked many comments ('Look at the biscuit tin drum!', 'I like making his football head', 'I like his cola tin shoes', 'Can I play the egg box now?', 'He's as big as the teacher!').

Differentiating the activity

To enable everyone in the group to participate in making the Music Man, very simple transformations can be made to create instruments: the children could make shakers from sealed and decorated yoghurt pots filled with pebbles or pulses; they could rub together two pieces of sandpaper; or use a wood block and beater.

Extension activities

● Show the children a teddy bear. Ask the children to look closely at its shape and then change the form of some clay, Plasticine or play dough to represent it.

● Change a jam jar lid and a bottle top into a candle holder for Divali celebrations. Glue the top upside down to the inside of the lid and decorate the base with pebbles, shells, flowers or small cones. Place clay or Plasticine inside the bottle top to hold a candle in place.

● More dextrous children could be given pieces of fabric and invited to make clothes for toys or bags or purses.

● More able children could be invited to create an Australian Aboriginal rainmaker. To make this you will need to cut out twelve cardboard tabs, 2 × 4 cm. Take two cardboard tubes, 8 cm in diameter by 24 cm in length, and ask the children to fix the tabs inside them with adhesive tape, three at each end, as far as their hands will reach.

Join the tubes together with adhesive tape to make one long tube. Put a cupful of rice inside the tube, then cover each end with paper taped securely in place to seal it.

Paint the outside of the tube in bright colours. Allow to dry, then slowly tip the tube from side to side to make the sound of rain.

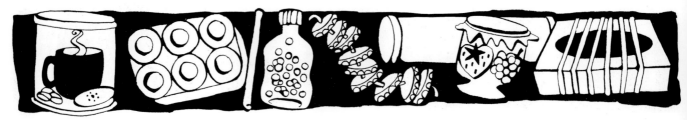

Involving parents

Encourage parents to allow the children to participate in creative activities at home that involve changing the form of materials, such as pottery, woodwork or needlework. Invite the parents into the classroom to help with the activities. Ask parents to save empty egg boxes, cardboard tubes, boxes and any other items that might be useful for modelling activities in the classroom.

Example

Madonna and Child
by Henry Moore

This particular statue was created for a church in Northampton in 1943. Moore's work generally provides excellent examples of techniques using marble, stone, wood, lead and wire.

Shape

Intended learning

To introduce the children to different shapes; for the children to recognise some shapes and to know the names of shapes; for them to be able to talk about objects in terms of their shapes; to use and discuss some shapes in two- and three-dimensional work.

> **Responding to:** *The Shape of Things* by Dayle Ann Dodds (Walker Books)
>
> See how a square is nothing more than a square – until, that is, a triangle is added for a roof, and oblongs are added for windows and a door! This book encourages children to look at and recognise the shapes around them and then use them effectively in their own art.

Key vocabulary

shape, square, oblong, triangle, circle, edges, corners

The activity

You will need:

a copy of *The Shape of Things* by Dayle Ann Dodds, examples of two- and three-dimensional shapes, card, scissors, glue, buttons, fabric scraps, coloured wool, old clothes, needle and thread, two sets of geometric shapes cut from plastic or card pen.

Points for discussion

● Share *The Shape of Things* together. Talk about how shapes differ and introduce the children to two-dimensional shapes, such as an oblong, square, triangle and circle. How many sides does each shape have? How many corners?

● Look together at a collection of objects from around the school with distinct geometric shapes (for example, a building brick, a ball, a musical triangle). Sort these into groups of objects containing circles, squares, oblongs and triangles.

After the discussion

Explain that the children are going to make a Shape Person. Help them to cut out a large triangle from card for the body, then glue on rectangles of card for arms. Make a circle head and square feet. Stick on brightly coloured wool for hair and buttons and fabric scraps for facial features. Let the children dress the Shape Person in old clothes and sew or stick on brightly coloured pockets.

Place plastic or thick card shapes, such as an oblong, square, triangle and circle, in the pockets. Display the Shape Person with a caption inviting the children to feel the shapes and try to guess what they are. For example:

I have in my pockets
As you can see
Lots of shapes
With sides 1, 4 and 3.
Can you tell me
What they might be?
I'll give you some clues,
Then you can help me.
One has four sides and they all look the same.
The second's a line that goes round like a train.
The third has two short sides and two that are long,
And the last could be rung like the bells in a song.

Provide extra shapes for the children to match up with the shapes in the pockets.

Finding the right shape to go in the right pocket

Assessment

● Can the children recognise and name the four basic shapes – oblong, square, triangle and circle?

● Can the children describe shapes?

● Do the children use these shapes in their art?

● Can they identify these shapes in other people's work?

Extension activities

● Children could draw round the four basic geometric shapes – circle, square, triangle and rectangle – to make pictures of cars, boats, houses, people, animals, etc.

Evidence of the children's learning

It was quite an occasion when the Shape Person was completed. Bindi was worried because they couldn't see his triangle body under his clothes, but found that she could feel the three sides quite easily through the clothing. The children enjoyed feeling the shapes in the pockets and telling their friends what they were. Katy found it easy to drop the shapes into the correct pocket.

Differentiating the activity

● Children can be encouraged to do simple jigsaw puzzles to help them recognise shapes and see how they can fit together.

● To reinforce the concept of shape, create sorting games using the four main shapes, and devise a 'Shape Snap Game' for children to play with a partner.

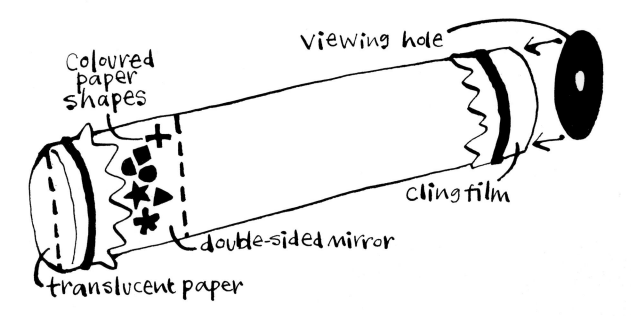

Coloured paper shapes

viewing hole

cling film

double-sided mirror

translucent paper

● Provide a kaleidoscope for children to observe changing shapes. Ask them to try to describe what shapes they can see.

A simple kaleidoscope could be made by rolling black card into a tube and securing it with adhesive tape, then wedging a double-sided mirror lengthways into one end. Cover the end of the tube with translucent paper such as greaseproof or thick tissue paper, secured with a rubber band or adhesive tape. Insert some brightly coloured paper shapes. Cover the other end with clingfilm to prevent the shapes from falling out. Glue a circle of card with a viewing hole cut in the centre over the cling-film. Encourage the children to shake the kaleidoscope to change the pattern made by the paper shapes.

● Use coloured pencils, wax crayons or felt-tipped pens to cover a large sheet of paper with random shapes to use as wrapping paper.

● Tear shapes from magazines or wallpaper to make a parrot collage. Give the parrot a round face and eyes, a rectangular body and a triangular beak and feathers. Stick it onto a rectangular perch on a square background.

● Drop an object into the water tray. Discuss the shapes that appear (ripples and concentric circles).

Involving parents

Encourage parents to point out shapes in the natural world, especially shadows on a sunny day. Ask parents to get their children to identify any shapes they can see in furniture and other objects around the home, for example, the rectangles of television and computer screens or the circles of saucepans and lids.

Example

Birds and Insects
by Joan Miró

This painting depicts images of shapeless insects surrounding a bird. The children could be invited to describe how known shapes have been used and distorted in the picture.

Looking at other artists

Intended learning

To observe the elements of art (line, colour, shape, tone, pattern, space, texture and form) as used in other people's art; for the children to be able to comment on what they see in other people's work; to begin to use the styles of artists in their own work.

> Responding to: *Berwick-on-Tweed* by L S Lowry
>
> Much can be gained by reproducing the style of a famous artist and can be easily accomplished by simplifying the main features. Here, Lowry's style is used as an example.

Key vocabulary

line, colour, tone, pattern, shape, space, texture, form, detail, painting, artist

The activity

You will need:

individual sketchbooks, a postcard of or a book containing a reproduction of Lowry's *Berwick-on-Tweed*, pipe cleaners, Plasticine, paper, painting equipment.

Points for discussion

● It can be difficult for young children to appreciate the overall shape of adults, buildings and other things in the environment around them. If possible, take the children to an elevated viewing point, such as a balcony or upstairs window, to look down on people from above and to make sketches. Discuss what they see.

● Back in the classroom, look together at the Lowry painting. Ask the children what they can see in the picture and encourage them to talk about it. Are there any interesting features? Encourage the children to look for specific aspects, such as the way the artist has painted the background or foreground.

● Encourage the children to look at how the artist has used the space on the paper. What colours has he used? Can they suggest which materials he used? Can they see any interesting shapes? Discuss any special techniques used by the artist, such as thick brush strokes.

● Talk about how the way in which Lowry has depicted people. Discuss the people's bent backs, the outstretched hands and the lack of facial features.

● Look at the children's sketches of what they saw from the elevated viewpoint. Talk about what they saw and how they could develop their sketches to make their own Lowry-style townscapes.

After the discussion

Give the children pipe cleaners or Plasticine and ask them to make their own matchstick people. Encourage them to imagine the people doing different things (shopping, running, working in the garden, etc.) and to alter their postures accordingly. Suggest that they make an animal, such as a horse or a dog, to include in their scene.

Encourage the children to arrange their figures to form a busy scene, as in the Lowry painting. Then ask them to try to draw or paint their scene using the same techniques and colours as Lowry. Remind them of the characteristic features they observed in the painting.

The children's work could be mounted and displayed together with the Lowry picture.

Naomi's picture of a Lowry-style market hall

Assessment

● Can the children make general observations about pictures?

● Can they identify specific features within the picture?

● Do they recognise any elements of art within the picture?

● Does their own work reflect that of other artists?

Evidence of the children's learning

The children were taken to view a busy indoor market scene from a balcony. There was a lot of movement created by the shoppers so they were asked to look especially for children, older people and stall-holders. They sketched people in their drawing books, taking particular notice of bent backs, raised arms and children in pushchairs. We decided together that the background stalls would be rectangular shapes. Naomi was excited to begin her picture and returned to it later to put in extra details.

Differentiating the activity

Many children will not have seen the work of famous artists before and will need to see them frequently and talk about them. Display a wide variety of art cards, posters and postcards in the classroom. Encourage children to find famous paintings in books and to talk about them.

Extension activities

● Make some Lowry-style houses by rolling out a slab of clay, then dividing it into unequal pieces. Give each child one piece with which to create a house shape. Let them use a blunt tool to add details before painting and varnishing their house. Fit the shapes together to make a plaque depicting a row of houses.

● Arrange a visit to a local art gallery. Many galleries have an education officer who will be able to organise activities according to the age and ability of your children.

● Show the children some reproductions of still life paintings, then encourage them to choose a familiar object and make a detailed observational drawing of it.

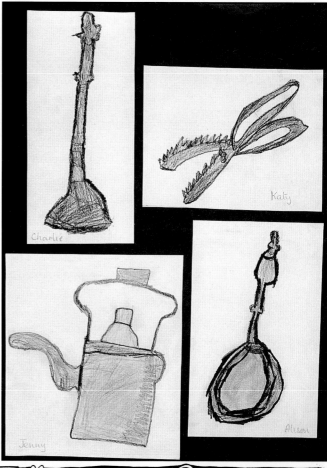

● Look at some examples of wallpapers and textiles designed by William Morris, then get the children to design some of their own.

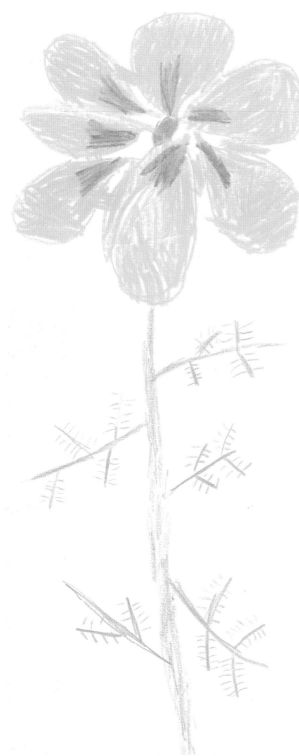

This flower picture was painted after a child had seen a reproduction of *Sunflowers* by Vincent van Gogh.

● Provide a range of examples of different kinds of art media to look at and discuss. Include sculptures and textiles as well as paintings.

● Look together at art from a range of cultures. Encourage the children to discuss the techniques and effects and then to adapt them for use in their own work.

● Get the children to draw and paint a landscape called 'By the Water'. This could show the sea, a pond, a river or a canal. Show the children some examples of pointillism (the use of coloured dots) as used by Georges Seurat. *A Sunday Afternoon on the Island of La Grande Jatte* is a good example. Suggest that they use the same technique for the background of their picture.

Involving parents

Make a collection of art postcards for parents to borrow and to talk about with their children. Ask parents to take their children to visit a local art exhibition or gallery, and to look at and discuss shop displays together.

Example

Various works of art

A number of books and packs offering a selection of reproductions of works of art are available (for example, *Art Packs* collated by Philip Green, published by Philip Green Educational Ltd).

Books featured in Art from stories, poems and songs

Book list

In the Garden, Susie Lacome (Walker Books)
When We Were Very Young, A A Milne (Methuen)
Skyfire, Frank Asch (Picture Corgi)
Little Penguin, Patrick Benson (Walker Books)
I Know Who Jesus Is, Helen Caswell
(The Lutterworth Press)
Elmer on Stilts, David McKee (Red Fox)
The Town Mouse and the Country Mouse
(Ladybird)
Thomas and the Lost Cat, Christopher Awdry
and Ken Stott (Heinemann)
The Circus, Brian Wildsmith (OUP)
The Three Little Pigs (Ladybird)
Honeybee's Busy Day, Richard Fowler
(Doubleday Press)
Okki-tokki-unga (A&C Black)
The Shape of Things, Dayle Ann Dodds
(Walker Books)

Useful addresses

Galt Educational (educational suppliers)
Culvert Street
Oldham
Lancs OL4 2GE

Hope Education (educational suppliers)
Orb Mill
Huddersfield Road
Oldham
Lancs OL4 2ST

Philip & Tacey Ltd (general educational
suppliers, but with a good range of art
materials)
North Way
Andover
Hants SP10 5BA

Philip Green Educational Ltd (educational
suppliers and publishers of the Art Packs)
112a Alcester Road
Studley
Warwickshire B80 7NR

Specialist Crafts Ltd (formerly Dryad,
suppliers of art and craft materials)
PO Box 247
Leicester LE1 9QS

Art and Craft magazine (a monthly
magazine of ideas for art activities in
infant and primary classrooms)
Scholastic Ltd
Villiers House
Clarendon Avenue
Leamington Spa
Warwickshire CV32 5LS

First published 1999 by A & C Black (Publishers) Ltd, 35 Bedford Row, London WC1R 4JH
Text copyright © Ann Malpass and Dorothy Tipton 1999. Illustrations copyright © Alison Dexter 1999.
All photographs copyright © Zul Mukhida 1999.
The authors wish to thank Tower House Nursery, Shrewsbury, Shropshire; Sue O'Donnell and her enthusiastic staff; St. Andrews C of E School, Nesscliffe, Shropshire; Balfour Infants School, Brighton; Jenny Parr; Diana Chadwick; Peter Malpass and John Tipton (for proof reading, coffee, support and encouragement).
ISBN 0-7136-4906-2
A CIP catalogue record for this book is available from the British Library.
Printed in Hong Kong through Colorcraft Ltd.